THE PSYCHICAL MECHANISM
OF FORGETFULNESS

BY

SIGMUND FREUD

British Library Cataloguing-in-Publication Data
A catalogue record for this book is available from the
British Library

Contents

Sigmund Freud

Sigismund Schlomo Freud was born on 6th May 1856, in the Moravian town of Příbor, now part of the Czech Republic.

Sigmund was the eldest of eight children to Jewish Galician parents, Jacob and Amalia Freud. After Freud's father lost his business as a result of the Panic of 1857, the family were forced to move to Leipzig and then Vienna to avoid poverty. It was in Vienna that the nine-year-old Sigmund enrolled at the Leopoldstädter Kommunal-Realgymnasium before beginning his medical training at the University of Vienna in 1873, at the age of just 17. He studied a variety of subjects, including philosophy, physiology, and zoology, graduating with an MD in 1881.

The following year, Freud began his medical career in Theodor Meynert's psychiatric clinic at the Vienna General Hospital. He worked there until 1886 when he set up in private practice and began specialising in "nervous disorders". In the same year he married Merth Bernays, with whom he had 6 children between 1887 and 1895.

In the period between 1896 and 1901, Freud isolated himself from his colleagues and began work on developing the basics of his psychoanalytic theory. He published *The Interpretation of Dreams*, in 1899, to a lacklustre reception, but continued to produce works such as *The Psychopathology of Everyday Life* (1901) and *Three Essays on the Theory of Sexuality* (1905). He held a weekly meeting at his home known as the "Wednesday Psychological Society" which eventually developed into the Vienna Psycho-Analytic Society. His ideas gained momentum and by the end of the decade his methods were being used internationally by neurologists and psychiatrists.

Freud made a huge and lasting contribution to the field of psychology with many of his methods still being used in modern psychoanalysis. He inspired much discussion on the wealth of theories he produced and the reactions to his works began a century of great psychological investigation.

In 1930 Freud fled Vienna due to rise of Nazism and resided in England until his death from mouth cancer on 23rd September 1939.

THE PSYCHICAL MECHANISM
OF FORGETFULNESS
(1898B)

The phenomenon of forgetfulness, which I should like to describe and then go on to explain in this paper, has doubtless been experienced by everyone in himself or been observed by him in others. It affects in particular the use of proper names - *nomen propria* - and it manifests itself in the following manner. In the middle of carrying on a conversation we find ourselves obliged to confess to the person we are talking to that we cannot hit on a name we wanted to mention at that moment, and we are forced to ask for his - usually ineffectual - help. 'What is his name? I know it so well. It's on the tip of my tongue. Just this minute it's escaped me.' An unmistakable feeling of irritation, similar to that which accompanies motor aphasia, now attends our further efforts to find the name, which we feel we had in our head only a moment before. In appropriate instances two accompanying features deserve our notice. First, an energetic deliberate concentration of the function which we call attention proves powerless, however long it is continued, to find the lost name. Secondly, in place of the name we are looking for, another name promptly appears, which we recognize as incorrect and reject, but which persists in coming back. Or else, instead of a substituted name, we find in our memory a single letter or syllable, which we. We say, for instance: 'It begins with a "B".' If we finally succeed, in one way or another, in discovering what the name is, we find in the great majority of cases that it does not begin with a 'B' and does not in fact contain the letter 'B' at all.

The best procedure for getting hold of the missing name is, as is generally known, 'not to think of it' - that is, to divert from the task that part of the attention over which one has voluntary control. After a while, the missing name 'shoots' into one's mind; one cannot prevent oneself from calling it out aloud - to the great astonishment of one's companion, who has already forgotten the episode and who has in any case only taken very little interest in the speaker's efforts. 'Really,' he is apt to say, 'it makes no difference *what* the man is called; only go on with your story.' The whole of the time until the matter is cleared up, and even after the intentional diversion, one feels preoccupied to a degree which cannot in fact be explained by the amount of interest possessed by the whole affair.[1]

In a few cases which I have myself experienced of forgetting names in this way, I have succeeded, by means of psychical analysis, in accounting to myself for the chain of events; and I shall now describe in detail the simplest and clearest case of this kind.

During my summer holidays I once went for a carriage drive from the lovely city of Ragusa to a town nearby in Herzegovina. Conversation with my companion centred, as was natural, round the condition of the two countries (Bosnia and Herzegovina) and the character of their inhabitants. I talked about the various peculiarities of the Turks living there, as I had heard them described years before by a friend and colleague who had lived among them as a doctor for many years. A little later, our conversation turned to the subject of Italy and of pictures, and I had occasion to recommend my companion strongly to visit Orvieto some time, in order to see the frescoes there of the end of the world and the Last Judgement, with which one of the chapels in the cathedral had been decorated by a great artist. But the artist's name escaped me and I could not recall it. I exerted my powers of recollection, made all the details of the day I spent in Orvieto pass before my memory and convinced myself that not the smallest part of it had been obliterated or become indistinct. On the contrary, I was able to conjure up the pictures with greater sensory vividness than is usual with me. I saw before my eyes with especial sharpness the artist's self-portrait - with a serious face and folded hands - which he has put in a corner of one of the pictures, next to the portrait of his predecessor in the work, Fra Angelico da Fiesole; but the artist's name, ordinarily so familiar to me, remained obstinately in hiding, nor could my travelling companion help me out. My continued efforts met with no success beyond bringing up the names of two other artists, who I knew could not be the right ones. These were *Botticelli* and, in the second place, *Boltraffio*.[2] The repetition of the sound 'Bo' in the two substitutive names might perhaps have led a novice to suppose that it belonged to the missing name as well, but I took good care to steer clear of that expectation.

[1] Nor by any feeling of unpleasure one may have at being inhibited in a psychical act.

[2] The first of these names was very familiar to me; the second, on the other hand, I hardly knew.

Since I had no access to any reference books on my journey, I had for several days to put up with this lapse of memory and with the inner torment associated with it which recurred at frequent intervals each day, until I fell in with a cultivated Italian who freed me from it by telling me the name: *Signorelli*. I was myself able to add the artist's *first* name, *Luca*. Soon my ultra-clear memory of the master's features, as depicted in his portrait, faded away.

What influences had led me to forget the name *Signorelli* which was so familiar to me and which is so easily impressed on the memory? And what paths had led to its replacement by the names *Botticelli* and *Boltraffio*? A short excursion back into the circumstances in which the forgetting had taken place sufficed to throw a light on both questions.

Shortly before I had come to the subject of the frescoes in the cathedral at Orvieto, I had been telling my travelling-companion something I had heard from my colleague years ago about the Turks in Bosnia. They treat doctors with special respect and they show, in marked contrast to our own people, an attitude of resignation towards the dispensations of fate. If the doctor has to inform the father of a family that one of his relatives is about to die, his reply is: '*Herr*, what is there to be said? If he could be saved, I know you would help him.' Another recollection lay in my memory close to this story. The same colleague had told me what overriding importance these Bosnians attached to sexual enjoyments. One of his patients said to him once: '*Herr*, you must know, that if *that* comes to an end then life is of no value.' At the time, it seemed to the doctor and me that the two character-traits of the Bosnian people illustrated by this could be assumed to be intimately connected with each other. But when I remembered these stories on my drive into Herzegovina, I suppressed the second one, in which the subject of sexuality was touched on. It was soon after this that the name *Signorelli* escaped me and that the names *Botticelli* and *Boltraffio* appeared as substitutes.

The influence which had made the name *Signorelli* inaccessible to memory, or, as I am accustomed to say, had 'repressed' it, could only proceed from the story I had suppressed about the value set on death and sexual enjoyment. If that was so, we ought to be able to discover the intermediate ideas which had served to connect the two themes. The affinity between their *content* - in the one case, the Last Judgement, 'Doomsday', and in the other, death and sexuality- seems to be very slight; and since the matter concerned the repression from memory of a *name*, it was on the face of it probable that the connection was between one name and another. Now, '*Signor*' means '*Herr*, and the '*Herr*' is also present in the name '*Her*zegovina'. Moreover it was certainly not without relevance that both the patients' remarks which I was to recall contained a '*Herr*' as a form of address to the doctor. The translation of '*Signor*' into '*Herr*' was therefore the means by which the story that I had suppressed had drawn after it into repression the name I was looking for. The whole process was clearly made easier by the fact that during the last few days in Ragusa I had been speaking Italian continually - that is, that I had become accustomed to translating German into Italian in my head.[1]

When I tried to recover the name of the artist, to bring it back out of repression, the influence of the tie which the name had entered into in the meantime inevitably made itself felt. I did find an artist's name, but not the right one. It was a displaced name, and the line of displacement was laid down by the names that were contained in the repressed topic. 'Bottic*elli*' contains the same final syllables as 'Signor*elli*';

the final syllables - which, unlike the first part of the word, '*Signor*', could not make a direct connection with the name 'Herzegovina' - had therefore returned; but the influence of the name 'Bosnia', which is regularly associated with the name 'Herzegovina', had shown itself by directing the substitution to two artists' names which began with the same syllable 'Bo': 'Botticelli' and then 'Boltraffio'. The finding of the name 'Signorelli' is thus seen to have been interfered with by the topic which lay behind it, in which the names 'Bosnia' and 'Herzegovina' appear.

¹ 'A far-fetched, forced explanation', it will be said. This impression to establish a connection with what is not suppressed; and for this purpose it does not scorn even the path of external association. There is the same 'forced' situation when rhymes have to be made.

For this topic to have been able to produce such effects it is not enough that I should have suppressed it once in conversation - an event brought about by chance motives. We must assume rather that the topic itself was also intimately bound up with trains of thought which were in a state of repression in me - that is, with trains of thought which, in spite of the intensity of the interest taken in them, were meeting with a resistance that was keeping them from being worked over by a particular psychical agency and thus from becoming conscious. That this was really true at that time of the topic of 'death and sexuality' I have plenty of evidence, which I need not bring up here, derived from my own self-investigation. But I may draw attention to one consequence of these repressed thoughts. Experience has taught me to require that every psychical product shall be fully elucidated and even overdetermined. Accordingly, it seemed to me that the second substitutive name, 'Boltraffio', called for a further determination; for so far only its initial letters had been accounted for, by their assonance with 'Bosnia'. I now recollected that these repressed thoughts had never engrossed me more than they had a few weeks before after I had received a certain piece of news. The place where the news reached me was called '*Trafoi*' and this name is too much like the second half of the name 'Boltraffio' not to have had a determining effect on my choice of the latter. In the following small schematic diagram, I have attempted to reproduce the relations which have now been brought to light.

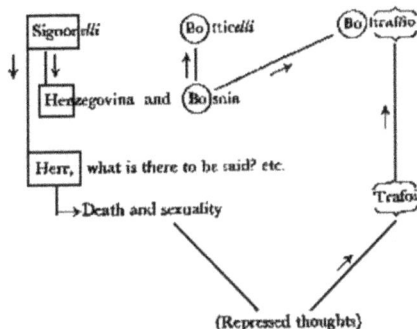

Fig. 1

It is perhaps not without interest for its own sake to be able to see into the history of a psychical event of this kind, which is among the most trivial disturbances that can affect the control of the psychical apparatus and which is compatible with an otherwise untroubled state of psychical health. But the example elucidated here receives an immensely added interest when we learn that it may serve as nothing more nor less than a model for the pathological processes to which the psychical symptoms of the psychoneuroses - hysteria, obsessions and paranoia - owe their origin. In both cases we find the same elements and the same play of forces between those elements. In the same manner as here and by means of similar superficial associations, a repressed train of thought takes possession in neuroses of an innocent recent impression and draws it down with itself into repression. The same mechanism which causes the substitute names 'Botticelli' and 'Boltraffio' to emerge from 'Signorelli' (a

11

substitution by means of intermediate or compromise ideas) also governs the formation of obsessional thoughts and paranoic paramnesias. Again, we have seen that such cases of forgetfulness have the characteristic of liberating continuous unpleasure till the moment the problem is solved - a characteristic which is unintelligible apart from this, and something which was in fact unintelligible to the person I was talking to; but there is a complete analogy to it in the way in which collections of repressed thoughts attach their capacity for producing affect to some symptom whose psychical content seems to our judgement totally unsuited to such a liberation of affect. Finally, the resolution of the whole tension by a communication of the correct name from an external quarter is itself a good example of the efficacy of psycho-analytic therapy, which aims at correcting the repressions and displacements and which removes the symptoms by re-instating the genuine psychical object.

Among the various factors, therefore, which contribute to a failure in recollection or a loss of memory, the part played by repression must not be overlooked; and it can be demonstrated not only in neurotics but (in a manner that is qualitatively the same) in normal people as well. It may be asserted quite generally that the ease (and ultimately the faithfulness, too) with which a given impression is awakened in the memory depends not only on the psychical constitution of the individual, the strength of the impression when it was fresh, the interest directed towards it at the time, the psychical constellation at the present time, the interest that is *now* devoted to its awakening, the connections into which the impression has been drawn, and so on - not only on such things but also on the favourable or unfavourable attitude of a particular psychical factor which refuses to reproduce anything that might liberate unpleasure, or that might subsequently lead to the liberation of unpleasure. Thus the function of memory, which we like to regard as an archive open to anyone who is curious, is in this way subjected to restriction by a trend of the will, just as is any part of our activity directed to the external world. Half the secret of hysterical amnesia is uncovered when we say that hysterical people do not know what they do not *want* to know; and psycho-analytic treatment, which endeavours to fill up such gaps of memory in the course of its work, leads us to the discovery that the bringing back of those lost memories is opposed by a certain resistance which has to be counterbalanced by work proportionate to its magnitude. In the case of psychical processes which are on the whole normal, it cannot, of course, be claimed that the influence of this one-sided factor in the revival of memories in any way regularly overcomes all the other factors that must be taken into account.[1]

[1] It would be a mistake to believe that the mechanism which
I have brought to light in these pages only operates in rare cases.

It is, on the contrary, a very common one. On one occasion, for instance, when I was meaning to describe the same small incident to a colleague of mine, the name of my authority for the stories about Bosnia suddenly escaped me. The reason for this was as follows. Just before, I had been playing cards. My authority was called Pick. Now '*Pick*' and '*Herz*' are two of the four suits in the pack. Moreover the two words were connected by an anecdote in which this same person pointed to himself and said: 'I'm not called "*Herz*", but "*Pick*".' '*Herz*' appears in the name '*Herzegovina*' and the heart itself, as a sick bodily organ, played a part in the thoughts I have described as having been repressed.

In connection with the tendentious nature of our remembering and forgetting, I not long ago experienced an instructive example - instructive because of what it betrayed - of which I should like to add an account here. I was intending to pay a twenty-four-hour visit to a friend of mine who unfortunately lives very far away, and I was full of the things I was going to tell him. But before this I felt under an obligation to call on a family of my acquaintance in Vienna, one of whose members had moved to the town in question, so as to take their greetings and messages with me to the absent relative. They told me the name of the *pension* in which he lived, and also the name of the street and the number of the house, and, in view of my bad memory, wrote the address on a card, which I put in my wallet. The next day, when I had arrived at my friend's, I began: 'I've only one duty to carry out that may interfere with our being together; it's a call, and it shall be the first thing I do. The address is in my wallet.' To my astonishment, however, it was not to be found there. So now I had to fall back on my memory, after all. My memory for names is not particularly good, but it is incomparably better than for figures and numbers. I may have been paying medical visits at a certain house for a year on end, and yet, if I should have to be driven there by a cab driver, I should have difficulty in remembering the number of the house. But in this case I had taken special note of the house number; it was ultra-clear, as if to jeer at me - for no trace remained in my recollection of the name of the *pension* or the street. I had forgotten all the data in the address which might have served as a starting - point for discovering the *pension*; and, quite against my usual habit, I had retained the number of the house, which was useless for the purpose. In consequence, I was unable to make the call. I was consoled remarkably quickly, and I devoted myself entirely to my friend. When I was back again in Vienna and standing in front of my writing desk, I knew without a moment's hesitation where it was that, in my 'absent-mindedness', I had put the card with the address on it. In my unconscious hiding of the thing the same intention had been operative as in my curiously modified act of forgetting.

www.ingramcontent.com/pod-product-compliance
Lightning Source LLC
Chambersburg PA
CBHW021724290326
41933CB00050B/1003